# First Ladies of the United States

# CROSSWORD PUZZLES

Carlisle, Massachusetts

First Ladies Crossword Puzzles



ISBN: 978-0-9882885-0-8

Published by
GRAB A PENCIL PRESS
an imprint of Applewood Books
Carlisle, Massachusetts 01741
www.grabapencilpress.com

10 9 8 7 6 5 4 3 2

Manufactured in the United States of America

# First Ladies of the United States

# CROSSWORD PUZZLES

The role of First Lady of the United States has changed dramatically since Martha Washington assumed the mantle of the nation's first First Lady. Our eighteenth- and nineteenth-century predecessors, for instance, would hardly have believed that a former First Lady could go on to enjoy her own political career. But Americans have since witnessed that very thing: Eleanor Roosevelt served as a spokesperson for the U.S. at the United Nations; Hillary Clinton has run for the highest political position—president of the United States.

Come learn more about the First Ladies and the influence they have had on the American nation. Discover how even the earliest of the nation's First Ladies exerted political influence. Abigail Adams shared her keen political insights with President John Adams. Dolley Madison worked behind the scenes and used her extensive social network to create valuable political allies for President James Madison.

In some respects, the job has remained remarkably the same. First Ladies have always used their prominent position to advocate for causes: women's suffrage, abolition of slavery, workers' rights, civil rights, health care . . . and the list goes on! Turn the page and learn for yourself how First Ladies have helped shape the nation and how the role itself has evolved through the years.

**PUZZLE ANSWERS ON BACK PAGES**

WHITE HOUSE HISTORICAL ASSOCIATION / WHITE HOUSE COLLECTION

# Martha Washington

**ACROSS**

1. As the first First Family, Martha and George Washington resided in both New York City and Philadelphia, the two temporary ___ of the United States.

4. Many admiring Americans fondly referred to the First Lady as ___ Washington.

6. After George Washington left the presidency, he and Martha retired to ___ ___, their farm in Virginia.

9. As the first First Lady, Martha initiated the practice of weekly ___ at the President's House, where she hosted elected officials, dignitaries, and the general public.

11. After the death of her husband in 1799, Martha Washington ___ all of their letters to each other.

13. Martha had four children, all of whom she ___.

**DOWN**

2. Martha freed her husband's ___ at Mount Vernon after his death.

3. Martha Washington was raised on a wealthy Virginia ___.

5. As a typical "society" girl, Martha's education consisted primarily of ___ and social skills.

But she was unusual in that she also learned to read and write.

7. A ___ during the Revolutionary War, George Washington was always joined by Martha at his winter encampments, including Valley Forge, Philadelphia, and Morristown.

8. Before her marriage to George Washington, Martha was ___ by Daniel Custis.

10. Martha Washington was a very private person; in describing her public role as First Lady, she wrote that she felt “more like a state ___ than anything else.”

12. In 1789 Martha Washington became the ___ First Lady of the United States.

WHITE HOUSE HISTORICAL ASSOCIATION / WHITE HOUSE COLLECTION

# Abigail Adams

**ACROSS**

2. Abigail and John Adams lived in a cottage at ___, a small town near Boston where they raised five children.

3. When the U.S. capital was moved from Philadelphia to Washington, Abigail became the first First Lady to reside in the __ __.

5. Abigail was not formally ___, but she was exceedingly well-read and considered a keen intellectual and an influential thinker.

8. John Adams, in a letter to his wife, first penned the famous quote, “Facts are ___ things.”

9. Abigail influenced the founding of the nation through her famous ___ to her husband, where she wrote of her ideas on government and politics.

12. In a 1776 letter to her husband, Abigail showed her support for the suffrage movement when she wrote, “If we mean to have Heroes, Statesmen and Philosophers, we should have learned ___.”

13. An early supporter of abolition, Abigail believed that ___ was evil and ran counter to the American ideal of liberty.

14. Considered by critics to be too influential as First Lady, Abigail was given the nickname Mrs. ___.

**DOWN**

1. Abigail lived in ___ during her husband’s French diplomatic service there.

4. Abigail was the ___ First Lady of the United States.

6. Abigail was born and raised in New ___, where her influential family was known for its prestigious line of Congregational ministers.

7. The letters between Abigail and John Adams offer a valuable glimpse into life and politics during the American ___ War.

8. Abigail was the mother of John Quincy Adams, the ___ president of the United States.

10. An outspoken advocate of women's ___, Abigail fought for girls to have the same educational opportunities as boys.

11. Abigail stayed at Braintree to run the farm and care for the children while John Adams served as a delegate for the Continental ___ in Philadelphia, Pennsylvania.

WHITE HOUSE HISTORICAL ASSOCIATION / WHITE HOUSE COLLECTION

# Dolley Madison

**ACROSS**

2. Born in 1768, Dolley was raised as a ___, a member of the Religious Society of Friends.

4. The Madisons retired to ___, their plantation in Virginia.

6. Dolley was forced to flee the White House during the ___ of 1812.

7. With her marriage to James Madison, her second marriage, Dolley made herself the center of Washington ___.

8. Considered the most influential woman in Washington society, Dolley helped the bachelor president Thomas Jefferson receive ladies at the White House—a job typically performed by the ___ ___.

10. Dolley's husband, James Madison, was the secretary of state for Thomas ___.

11. The White House was in a ruined state after the ___ of Washington, and the Madisons had to find temporary housing upon their return to the city.

12. Dolley established her social and political influence in the ways that were traditionally available to women: letter writing, hostessing social events, and ___ with women who were married to influential politicians.

**DOWN**

1. Dolley met Representative ___ Madison in Philadelphia and they were married in 1794.

3. Dolley was the ___ First Lady of the United States.

5. Dolley's ___ savvy matched her renowned social graces, and her behind-the-scenes diplomacy was greatly prized by President Madison.

8. Dolley's first husband was the victim of a yellow ___ epidemic, leaving her widowed with a young son named Payne.

9. During the War of 1812, as the British troops approached the city of Washington, Dolley famously refused to leave the White House until she had ensured the rescue of George Washington's famous ___.

WHITE HOUSE HISTORICAL ASSOCIATION / WHITE HOUSE COLLECTION

# Julia Tyler

**ACROSS**

4. Julia scandalized her parents by allowing a drawing of her likeness to be used in an ___ for a clothing store; a young, unmarried woman of the elite upper class was expected to remain away from the public eye.

5. Julia married the ___ president, John Tyler, in 1844.

9. Even though Julia was born and raised in New York, she supported the ___ throughout the Civil War.

10. Julia was famously known as the "___ of Long Island."

11. Julia agreed to a ___ engagement with President Tyler after he stayed by her side while she grieved her father.

12. Julia attended the Madame N. D. Chagaray Institute for Young Ladies in New York City, a ___ school for girls from very wealthy families.

**DOWN**

1. The Tylers retired from the White House to ___ ___, in Virginia.

2. Julia is the first known First Lady to ever publicly ___ in the White House.

3. During an outing aboard the *Princeton* with President Tyler, Julia's ___ was killed by an accidental explosion.

6. After the South's defeat in the Civil War, Julia, then widowed, lost the Virginia ___ and all of her wealth.

7. During her grand tour of Europe as a young woman, Julia was impressed by the formalities of ___ tradition; as First Lady she emulated this regal formality.

8. Toward the end of her life, after living years in poverty as a widow, Julia successfully petitioned ___ for an annual stipend of $1200.

WHITE HOUSE HISTORICAL ASSOCIATION / WHITE HOUSE COLLECTION

# Mary Todd Lincoln

**ACROSS**

2. Mary was the daughter of ___ who settled in Kentucky.

3. The position of First Lady during the ___ ___ was a delicate one for Mary because she grew up in the South and was considered a traitor by many there.

4. Mary successfully petitioned ___ for the establishment of a presidential widow's pension.

5. When Abraham Lincoln met his future bride, he was, in his own words, “a ___ nobody.”

6. Mary was unusually ___ ___; she learned to read and write French and studied literature, poetry, astronomy, and geography in addition to the etiquette training that was more typical for young wealthy ladies.

7. President Lincoln and Mary Lincoln’s son, Willie, suffered a sudden and tragic ___ during the family’s tenure in the White House.

9. Mary believed in the full emancipation of ___.

**DOWN**

1. The 1865 ___ of President Lincoln left Mary heartbroken.

5. Mary actively promoted her husband’s ___ career by letter writing, advising, and attending important political events.

8. Mary worked as a volunteer ___ in Union hospitals.

WHITE HOUSE HISTORICAL ASSOCIATION / WHITE HOUSE COLLECTION

# Frances Cleveland

**ACROSS**

4. Frances and Grover Cleveland were married in the ___ ___.

6. Frances hosted two weekly receptions at the White House, one on Saturdays for women who ___ during the week.

7. ___ was Frances's nickname.

8. Before President Grover Cleveland wed Frances, he spent his first fifteen months in office as a ___.

9. The public was fascinated by the new First Lady, and ___ were quick to use her image on every sort of product imaginable.

11. The Clevelands enjoyed two ___ terms in the White House.

**DOWN**

1. Shortly after their marriage, Frances joined her husband on his famous 1887 tour of the ___.

2. After marrying Frances, President Cleveland purchased a large farm in an area of Washington, D.C., later named ___ ___.

3. Before President Cleveland married Frances, his unmarried sister Rose fulfilled the duties of ___ ___.

4. Frances graduated from Wells College, one of the first colleges established for ___ in the United States.

5. Frances was very popular as First Lady, and the nation took keen interest in Esther, the only Cleveland child ___ during their time at the White House.

7. Grover Cleveland was the business partner of Frances's ___.

10. Grover and Frances Cleveland lived mostly on their farm, Red Top, and occupied the White House only during the ___ season.

WHITE HOUSE HISTORICAL ASSOCIATION / WHITE HOUSE COLLECTION

# Eleanor Roosevelt

**ACROSS**

1. Although considered radical in the 1930s, Eleanor publicly supported equal rights for ___ Americans.

3. As First Lady, Eleanor wrote a daily syndicated ___ column titled "My Day."

6. Eleanor worked as a teacher at a settlement house, a place dedicated to the improved living conditions of the ___ poor.

8. Eleanor presided as First Lady during the Great ___ and the Second World War.

10. The New York estate of Franklin and Eleanor is called ___ ___.

12. Eleanor was an active member in the women's division of the ___ Democratic Committee.

13. Eleanor served as an American spokesperson in the United ___.

**DOWN**

2. Eleanor had major apprehensions about becoming First Lady and how it might limit her own ___ and political commitments.

4. Active in the social reform movement of the ___ Era, Eleanor fought for the rights of women and the working class.

5. During WWII, Eleanor made sure that the White House adhered to the same food and gas ___ restrictions as the rest of the country.

7. Eleanor was the niece of the twenty-sixth president, ___ Roosevelt.

9. At the age of nine, Eleanor became an ___ and went to live with her grandmother.

11. Eleanor was the first First Lady to hold her own ___ conferences.

WHITE HOUSE HISTORICAL ASSOCIATION / WHITE HOUSE COLLECTION

# Jacqueline Kennedy

**ACROSS**

3. During the last two decades of her life, Jacqueline lived in New York City and worked for Doubleday as a book ___.

7. As First Lady Jacqueline made it known that her top priority was the well-being of her ___.

8. Although she never did write a ___, as a young woman Jacqueline had ambitions to be an author.

11. Jacqueline convinced her newly elected husband to invite prominent artists to his ___ as a demonstration of their support of the arts.

## DOWN

1. Jacqueline founded the White House ___ Association, an organization dedicated to public education and the preservation of the White House collections.

2. When Jacqueline first met ___ Kennedy, she was working at the *Washington Times-Herald* as a photographer.

4. Jacqueline showed her support of the Civil Rights movement when she publicly released photographs of the ___ kindergarten she had started at the White House.

5. A ___ icon, her unique style was copied by designers and women across America.

6. Jacqueline was a leading proponent for the creation of a national center for arts, named the ___ ___.

9. With the help of a committee and restoration experts, Jacqueline turned the White House into a ___ of American history and decorative arts.

10. Jacqueline was the first First Lady to have her own __ secretary.

WHITE HOUSE HISTORICAL ASSOCIATION / WHITE HOUSE COLLECTION

# Betty Ford

**ACROSS**

3. Betty was a strong and vocal supporter of the ___ Rights Amendment.

8. Betty helped to form the ___ Women's Federal Forum, a group that exchanged ideas on legislation and party issues.

11. Betty became the First Lady in 1974 upon the resignation of President ___.

12. Betty was especially adept at ___ for her husband, Gerald Ford.

**DOWN**

1. While in the White House Betty talked ___ about fighting breast cancer and created an important new awareness of the disease and its prevention.

2. Betty Ford was unique in her public support of causes that were not supported by the administration—for instance, federally funded ___ ___ for children.

4. As First Lady, Betty championed the arts as well as the rights of persons with ___.

5. Open about her struggle to overcome alcohol and drug ___, Betty helped to establish the Betty Ford Center for the treatment of substance abuse.

6. In 1975 Betty was named ___ of the Year by *Time* magazine.

7. Betty organized a dance group of her own while also ___ dance to disabled children.

9. Betty was awarded the Presidential ___ of Freedom in 1991 by George H. Bush and the Congressional Gold Medal in 1999 by Bill Clinton.

10. After graduating from college, Betty was a ___ in a noted New York City performance group.

WHITE HOUSE HISTORICAL ASSOCIATION / WHITE HOUSE COLLECTION

# Nancy Reagan

**ACROSS**

3. Nancy majored in ___ at Smith College and went on to act in both plays and movies.

6. Nancy and her husband, ___ Reagan, were both in the movie *Hellcats of the Navy.*

7. Nancy was central in the creation of the Ronald Reagan Library and has since encouraged the use of the library for Republican presidential ___.

10. For many years Nancy promoted the Foster ___ program, which paired the elderly from state institutions and children with disabilities.

11. Nancy's favorite color was ___, calling it a "picker-upper" and she wore it accordingly.

**DOWN**

1. Before Nancy was the First Lady of the United States, she was the First Lady of ___.

2. Nancy's Just Say No program aimed to keep children and young adults from experimenting with ___.

4. The first First Lady to address the U.N. General Assembly, Nancy spoke about the dangers and effects of international drug ___.

5. The Nancy Reagan Foundation promoted awareness of the dangers of ___.

8. Nancy Reagan sought to restore glamour and ___ to the White House and had great interest in iconic, high-end fashion.

9. When her husband was diagnosed with Alzheimer's disease, Nancy volunteered much of her time to the Alzheimer's Association and helped to establish the Ronald and Nancy Reagan ___ Institute.

WHITE HOUSE HISTORICAL ASSOCIATION / WHITE HOUSE COLLECTION

# Hillary Clinton

**ACROSS**

1. Hillary spearheaded the Save America's ___ program, which provides financial support to institutions that preserve historically important objects and places.

5. While First Lady, Hillary served as head of the National Commission on ___ ___ Reform.

7. After graduating from Wellesley College, Hillary went on to earn her juris doctor at Yale ___ School.

8. Hillary met her future husband, ___, while at Yale.

10. Bill and Hillary settled in Arkansas, where he became the ___ in 1978.

12. As a high school student, Hillary was a member of the National ___ Society.

**DOWN**

2. Barack Obama appointed Hillary to his cabinet as secretary of ___.

3. Hillary wrote two ___ books: *It Takes a Village* and *Other Lessons Children Teach Us.*

4. In 2016 Hillary ran for ___.

6. Hillary was the first First Lady to go on to be elected to ___.

9. Hillary helped to create Vital Voices, a program that promoted the participation of ___ from all over the world in their nation's politics.

11. Hillary was the only First Lady to have an ___ in the West Wing, along with the president's most senior staff.

WHITE HOUSE PHOTOGRAPH

# Michelle Obama

**ACROSS**

2. Together Michelle and Barack created Let Girls Learn, a program meant to empower girls around the world by helping them go to ___.

5. In keeping with her commitment to community service, as First Lady Michelle created a national ___ service program.

6. Before becoming ___ ___, Michelle worked at the University of Chicago, where she was an associate dean of student services and the vice president of community and external affairs.

9. Michelle was dedicated to building a career based upon community ___.

10. In high school Michelle was invited to join the National Honor Society and served as treasurer on the student ___.

**DOWN**

1. Michelle's program Let's Move! was created to address the childhood obesity epidemic and promote ___ living.

3. In addition to working full-time and raising two daughters, Michelle also ___ for her husband.

4. Michelle is the first ___ ___ First Lady.

7. After graduating from Princeton University, Michelle went on to earn a ___ degree from Harvard University.

8. Michelle joined a law firm in Chicago, where she was assigned to be an adviser to ___ Obama.

10. Michelle was born and raised in ___, Illinois.

# PUZZLE ANSWERS

## Martha Washington

## Abigail Adams

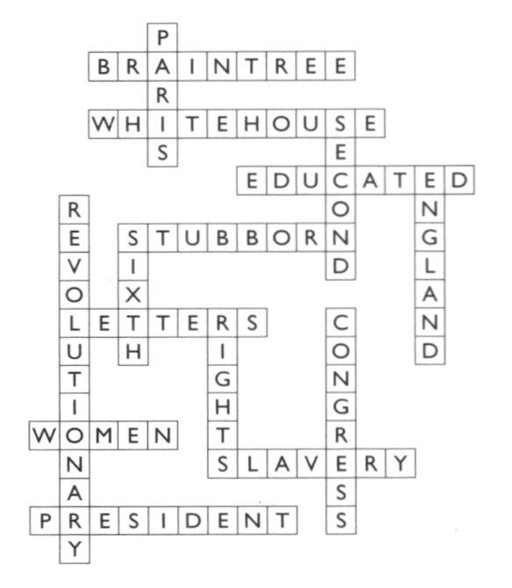


## Dolley Madison

## Julia Tyler

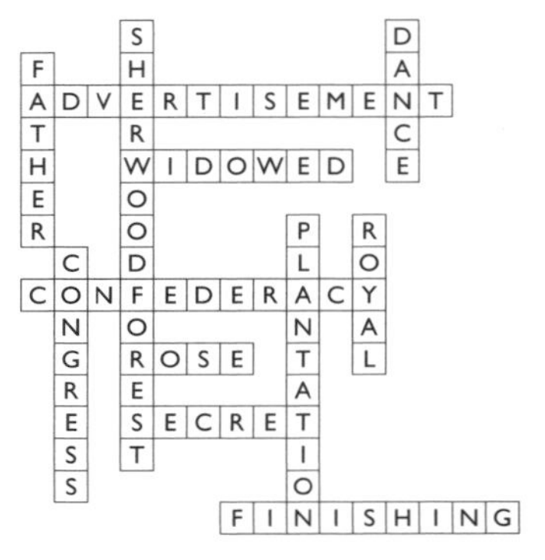

## Mary Todd Lincoln

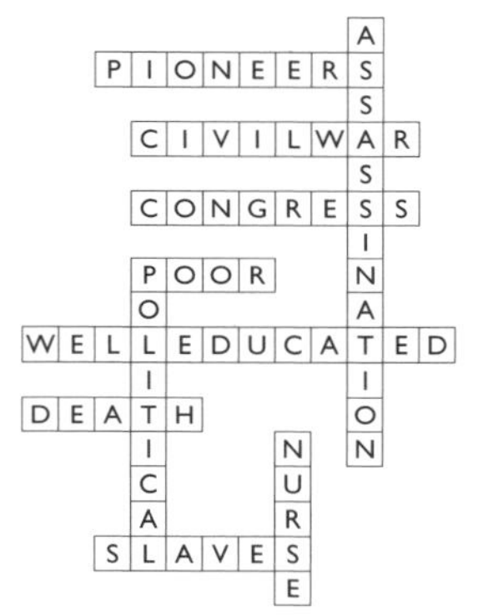


## Frances Cleveland

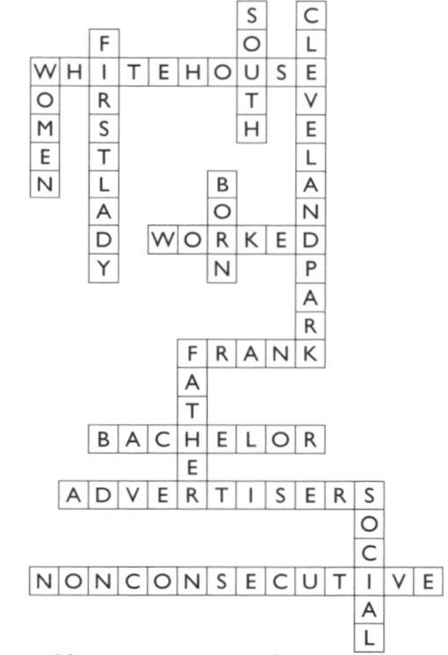


## Eleanor Roosevelt

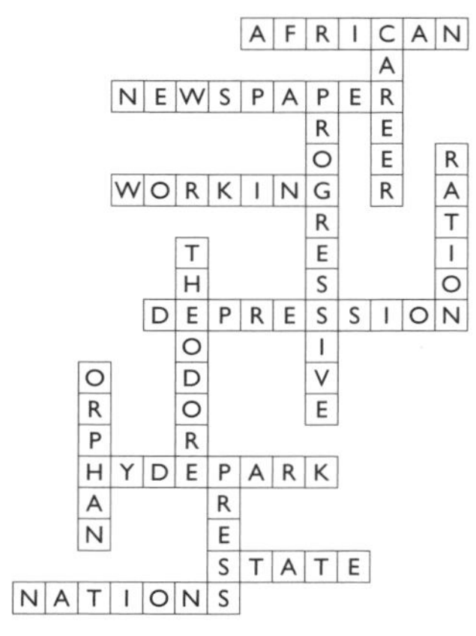


## Jacqueline Kennedy

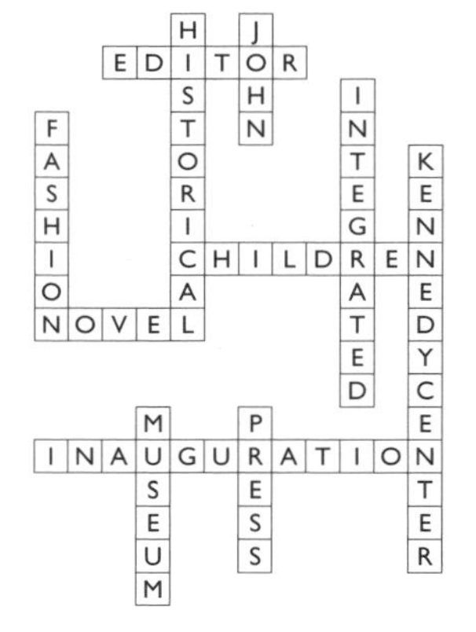

# Betty Ford

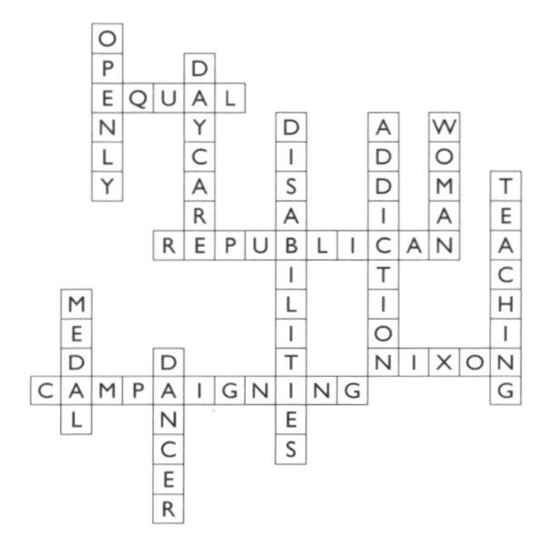


# Nancy Reagan

# Hillary Clinton

# Michelle Obama

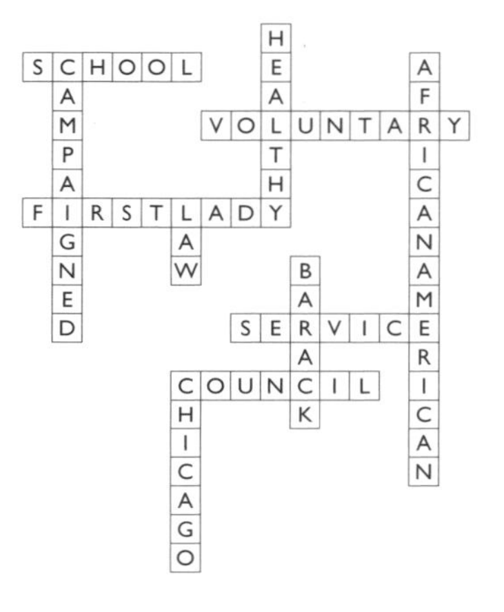

TOPICS

# GRAB A PENCIL PRESS

Abraham Lincoln
American Flag
American Revolution
Architecture
Art History
Benjamin Franklin
Civil War History
Ellis Island and the Statue of Liberty
First Ladies
George Washington
John Fitzgerald Kennedy
National Parks
Natural History
New York City
Presidents of the United States
Texas History
Vietnam War
Washington, D.C.
World War II
World War II European Theater
World War II Pacific Theater
Yellowstone National Park

**COMING SOON**

Flight Puzzle Book
Korean War Puzzle Book
Library of Congress Puzzle Book
Secret Writing: A Code Breaker's Puzzle Book

USA GRAB A PENCIL PRESS

*an imprint of Applewood Books*
*Carlisle, Massachusetts 01741*
www.grabapencilpress.com

To order, call: 800-277-5312